# Clowns & Acrobats

SEAMUS CASHMAN comes from the village of Conna in County Cork. Educated at the local primary school where his father was 'The Master', and at St Colman's College, Fermoy, he also studied for the priesthood at Maynooth College but left after three years. Having obtained a higher diploma in education at University College Cork, he spent some 'glorious years' in the mountains of southern Tanzania learning and teaching. He subsequently taught in Ireland before joining Irish University Press as an editor. He founded what was to become one of Ireland's premier literary and cultural publishing houses, Wolfhound Press, in 1974. He lives in Portmarnock, County Dublin.

*By the same author*

---

*Carnival* (poetry) (Monarchline, 1988)

*Proverbs & Sayings of Ireland.* With Sean Gaffney (Wolfhound Press, 1974, current edition 1996)

*The Wolfhound Book of Irish Poems for Young People.* With Bridie Quinn (Wolfhound Press, 1975; current edition 1990)

# Clowns & Acrobats

## Seamus Cashman

First published in 2000 by
Wolfhound Press Ltd
68 Mountjoy Square
Dublin 1, Ireland
Tel: (353-1) 874 0354
Fax: (353-1) 872 0207

© 1999 Seamus Cashman

All rights reserved. No part of this book may be reproduced or utilised in any form or by any means digital, electronic or mechanical including photography, filming, video recording, photocopying, or by any information storage and retrieval system or shall not, by way of trade or otherwise, be lent, resold or otherwise circulated in any form of binding or cover other than that in which it is published without prior permission in writing from the publisher.

British Library Cataloguing in Publication Data
A catalogue record for this book is available from the British Library.

ISBN 0-86327-744-6 (paperback)
ISBN 0-86327-768-3 (hardback)

Cover Design: Eva Byrne
Typesetting: Wolfhound Press
Typeset in Adobe Garamond $\frac{11.5}{15}$
Printed in the Republic of Ireland by Techman, Dublin.

# Contents

| | |
|---|---|
| Sacred Places | 9 |
| Is this how the gods were made? | 10 |
| Poem on a Sinday morning | 11 |
| Homage to a Dead Jellyfish | 13 |
| The Execution of Lady Jane Grey | 15 |
| Flying a Kite | 17 |
| Holding Hands | 19 |
| The Lotus Blossom and the Rose | 20 |
| I Was Afraid to Begin | 21 |
| The Mask | 22 |
| Diptych | 24 |
| For Grace, A Visitor | 26 |
| Journey | 28 |
| My Brother's Room | 29 |
| On a Train To New York City | 30 |
| On the steps at New York Public Library | 32 |
| Metropark, New Jersey | 33 |
| A Daddy Bewildered | 34 |
| My Treat | 35 |
| Bird in a Vacuum Pump | 36 |
| Child Asleep | 37 |
| Wordwaiting | 39 |
| A Final Fling | 40 |
| Lutan Baba | 42 |
| The Seven Masks of Tone LaGee | 44 |

| | |
|---|---:|
| Cursor | 46 |
| Versifying Verses 1–4 | 48 |
| When a Friend died ... | 50 |
| Remembering Daddy | 52 |
| Great Hungry Poets | 54 |
| In a stormy place | 55 |
| The Whole Universe is up for Grabs | 57 |
| The Stoker on the Rim | 59 |
| The Man who tried to sell Dublin to the Bolsheviks | 61 |
| While you were Out there | 63 |
| I Think My Mind Can Blossom | 65 |
| Clown Faces | 67 |
| Carnival Clowns & Acrobats | 68 |

*Soracha, Fergus, Cormac, Aideen*

for all you still teach me on the sidelines

## Sacred Places

They buried
warm bones and juicy flesh
deep in their soil
for four thousand years

and piled upon their memories
granite boulders, quartz and clay
garnered from the scrotums
and the breasts of distant places.

Their couplings faded into death
and left us sacred places to regret or visit,
places to dispel our slipping times and ages
for memory's imagination.

*Come o holy spirit, fill the hearts of us —*
*breathe on us immortality.*

Once I stole a stone
from such a sacred place.

And when I hold it to my soul
I find within its momentary chill
the warmth of history.

Some day I will go back
and surreptitiously return it
to its place in time.

Some day in my time
I will establish my own place
free of worship
full of hope.

# Is this how the gods were made?

Is this how the gods were made?
That you should fall with such a noise
the whole world would notice and remember.
And the devils too?

This is surely how the gods were made:
— a thunder clap, a lightening strike,
markers on our minds.
Like childhood, time indulged;
indelible, intricate, certain.

Yet, you too seem like a god among us
gently tiny, timidly filling spaces
left untenanted by all our greater gods
and giving sometimes joy
and grip to our uncertainties.

# Poem on a Sinday morning

*A blade from Lu Hsun's* Wild Grass

Stripped naked and grasping sharpened knives
they crouch in confrontation
pounding dust with bare feet thumps that dance
and pounce and jump about
now back to back, now facing,
pause rigid, atrophy;
their eyes hook deep into each other's memory
their bodies ready for their hate.

Squat man. Squat woman. They were lovers.
He tongued that palm that now held death
white-knuckled in its fury
and seeped into those open pores
his very being till he felt and thought that they were one.
Síle-na-gig she taunts his with, and Shiva — and those
    hook-eyes
tearing at his soul clench his fists now
and render him erect.

Squat man. Squat woman. Mating pair.
She palmed that tongue that held her thrall
that frightened her perception of herself and thrilled inside
her melting bones and flesh and slid through his and fused.
Challenged by those knowing pupils scanning hers she tensed
no longer soft, no longer thralled
she knew her ground.

They held this finite pose unable to undo their loves,
    unwilling to unlock their eyes

believing in some greater power to clothe their souls,
tasting on their tongues the blood that they might spill. Nor could they kill
nor could they choose their moves.

From radiant roads and laneways came the passers-by
rushing neat and clean and busy through the city to fulfil
the work. Some craned their necks to see
the naked waiting mid the crossing streets. Some questioned why.
And through their day
they wondered at the bloodtaste on their tongues. And in the night
the quiet gave them sleep.

## Homage to a Dead Jellyfish

'Would anybody call you Beautiful?' I asked a dead jellyfish
   on a cold morning — Saturday — in January,
   halfway along Portmarnock beach.

The opening sky rose behind Ireland's Eye,
   turning chunkiness into 2-D
   blackness, flattened halfway out at sea.

High overhead a pair of cloud-9 clouds perched
   lowly in the yellowing silence, hovering, uncertain.
   No wind. Nowhere else to go.

Quite suddenly, a glowing rim of intense ochre peered
   above the island hub. Surprise.
   I raised my arm to time its levitation.

Two minutes and five seconds saw this halo-hallowed-shimmer clear
   the island spine,
   free of earth and resurrected.

I never thought the universe could move so fast.

Now that was Beautiful. And the dead Jellyfish
   hadn't noticed. It was dead of course.
   I toe'd it over to discover underneath
   A rudimentary tentacle or something in its middle.
   And mouth-like orifices by the rim
   conducting star-form musculature
   to a barely opaque gut.
   For feeding?

I humped it back again and washed the crystal dome with
 wave.
 Then squat and watched and saw what I had missed
 before —
 its mauves and violets, blushing
 four domed-patterns to the rim.

My eye fixed on the creature's heavy immobility, hoping
 for some sign.
 My finger traced its boundaries in the sand.

A shadow rose beside me to the dunes. I strode
 to fill my walk watching its distortions
 ripple on the beach.

'Poor Jellyfish,' it sighed aloud,
 and gave me smiles, and told me
 look up to the clouds.

## The Execution of Lady Jane Grey

What would you choose to contemplate,
those early final hours before the chop?
Sweet skinned girl. That painter loved
who surely satisfied his patron
centuries ago, beyond this mind.

Bewitched by whites of gown and skin
shining from a darker past
I frowned inside as lookers smiled
at my spine's involuntary twitch.
I bent to tug a shoelace, hide a face.

I slid into your ache.
How grim to welcome death
all here gone, all there unknown
or in your stakes — child of power
could you have known? — did game plays
numb the end, and knowledge fail?
Nine days a Queen — 'tis just a joke
a merry-go-round, a summer sail.

Was that some noble Chancellor manipulating time
or fearful uncle brave to touch?
How elegant the wine tight trows and latticed jet
of this fine high solemn executioner.
His hatchet sharp and heavy
knives and ropes and death
all set to implement the State

Good god child, look at you!
How lovely:

Puberty and state have just abandoned you
and left you ripe for loving.
Yet this is all.

Sisters feint and faintly cry their agonies;
one turns her back
for shame perhaps —
one holds remorse.
You seem to spread
voluptuously for dying
in that young
white silken gown
of melting folds.

You let his palms enfold with strength
to lay your neck against the block
your golden hair untainted yet,
the block new hewn for blooding Jane.
A painterly romance upon a cushion.

On February the twelfth they murdered you
in fifteen thirty four.
Who four centuries beyond would
talk with you and hope to find a touch
before your time had had its day?

Is it too too late to pray?

## Flying a Kite

Flying a kite with you on the green green grass of home.
Do you remember your instant energetic joy
when I ask if you liked kites?

Last night my dream was filled
with the kind of romance
that I had thought long channelled
into song and otherworld nostalgia.
An aria for one forgotten love
now surfacing discreetly through your image
to stir my bone.

Last night I rose like Christ ascending from deep sleep
to slip untrammelled through the speeding skies above
and in a world of primary clarities
and found below your girl-like figure dancing
singing, slowly skipping on a broad green meadow-field
with undulating undetermined margins.
In one upstretched hand a string on which
your beauty hovered high beside me
as a kite on glorious spreading wings, firm-set upon the
    wind.
I moved to touch its colours with my palm
and paused to rest upon its glowing seals
and butterflies and peacock discs and chinese-dragoned
    spine.
I thought it was my soul's sin weight upon you
that brought us down in waft and wave and waft
until your kite with me upon it

reached you on the ground, and in your arm
I found its strong and gory string
full wound about your palm
and in your eyes the searching silver I must mine.
Nor had I thought that there could be a kite so beautiful
that it would joy my love in sleep and leave my mornings
high on dream.

## Holding Hands

I took your hands to say I love you
but my words were crude, unlike me, unworthy of you
and of all womanhood
I must ask myself — and I have, I have —
Is chauvinism bred so deep?
that what I think to be a lifetime consciousness
by instinct anti all that sad male need that hides
us from ourselves and makes us weak not strong
is no more than a shell cherished
deeper than the flesh beneath.

I well remember when the good news came
confirming my beliefs of womanhood, manhood,
my surprise that this should be any wonder, any issue.
That I knew was ignorance — to be reveined.

A mate's assertiveness, and more, her rightness
sliced from my tongue a plethora of maleword scum,
left me never unaware again. And now — a decade on
I take your hand to say I love you
and I do such wrong.

When you withdrew your touch, so now, so quick
so easily, I could not breach the silence
for my memory had found your love
and searched my life
and lost your hand.

Odd times I cup my palm into that clasp
and breath your spirit deep
and know you are away.

And wish for Cleopatra's asp.

## The Lotus Blossom and the Rose

I had never held a lotus plant
nor smelled its perfume, touched its petals;
but I knew it would be beautiful
and perfumed with a velvet touch
for it was what I thought of ...

I have seen and tasted roses
(grown them too)
and crushed their petals in my palms
releasing juices full of you.
I hope to taste some day the sweetness ...

I dream of swimming at the edge
plunging with the power of waterfall
deep in the swirling pool
that threads our waters to the womb.

# I Was Afraid to Begin

I was afraid to begin
— pen in hand, notebook open
desk lamp on, rain outside.

There were noises downstairs.
I went to check.
Tyre screeches pierced my window pane.
I looked out.
I went to pee. I went to see. I went to be
doing something else.

What was it feared?
ignorance, or jest;
words upon this window pane;
discovery, or nothingness?
I was afraid to begin
so I made it a first line.

# The Mask

Relentlessly, I search,
my hold-all sporting innocence,
for the mask I cannot find.
A mask for my magnificence
to wear in paradise.

I see it now, this super gear
the shadow of a lion eating sugared almonds
effigies of Nero and Napoleon
Christ beside some Cross
a woman wearing eardrop emeralds
with golden skin and eyes of blue enamel, silver painted
    pupae
on each cheek, death's head moth her mouth.
I lose her face distracted by demanding breast
and fingertouch
... and so it is I see.

There are passages within each eye
leading to extraordinary arches of the mind.
I season both, my eyes
absorbing blood-rimmed catacombs within;
enveloped, drawn, I spiral arms and feet full stretched.

Here is destiny — just near my touch, so near ...
and through its sphinctered arch
a half soul I have chaffed,
busy busy with some casual certitude;
and here beneath this glorious triumph
to some brute man

a gentle energy I well remember —
foolishly abandoned — aah!
We seldom solemnise our truth.

I see this woman reft in two, rising from those caves
my left eye finding in her right-eyed cavern
the severed right-hand side, and in her left,
a matching severed left.
My eyes can not re-form disjointed body
with disjointed soul.
I turn away.

If I could place each semi-vision
to the trim, beyond the margins
of my life, could she and I survive
such pages of design unedited?
Perhaps I should divide and set my severed shapes
upon the verso ... and recreate a pair of balanced souls.
My passion dissipates and as I ride in envy
with her ecstasy, her eyes and mine disintegrate
and I am left alone watching an unlit candle
set in ornamental horn, and a basket of bread.

My great mask is here and it fills my dread
with simple fear. What if it won't come off?
Putting on is not the question:
the now; to do; to be.
Consequences terrify me —
so close to paradise, so close to hell.

## Diptych

I watched apart, my body
mirror at your window misted pane
and saw it fade into our morning light
my sole remains a shadow on your glass.

You tissued tears away from me.
The past is broken ground,
trampled close, beaten down.

When I returned, I was amazed to find
my lost reflection, crystal true —

I thought perhaps if I should repossess that place
and pose to my reflection, it could restore me,
I could save face.

Like a broken photograph remade
isolated, complimentary images
no artificial eye enforming my regeneration;
juxtaposed coincidence
the jetsam of discarded consciousness.

A shift in time and place.
Your window — and my body image there —
traps you, traps me.
Perhaps those tears were for release
[though I think not]
I have in mind a diptych:

naked woman standing high, her head thrown back
eyes eating through the sky. Upstretched, outstretched arms
palm front, cry power in her possession of herself.

Her strong and slender body, nippled sure and pubic
 bushed.
Her legs apart, cut-off mid-knee to join
two upturned trunks of slender solid bushy trees.
There it is! Three points of note:
her power; her bushiness; her trees.

I thought I'd try that pose for me
but wisdom intervened ... damn it.
Find an obstacle and mask it;
find a hole through your maze of wall
a ramp hinged to your obsessions;
plant a tree with roots that seek
the centre of the earth and spreading foliage
to shelter shadow. Reach with your hands
and hold the sky to ransom for your future.
Touch your woman/man, and taste your being.

## For Grace, A Visitor

To reach you we sped on highways, turnpikes, byroads tree possessed,
and wooden villages. We were late. But so were you. In tears.
I wondered if my presence would embarrass;
your family must question my inclusion — though not to me.

You talked
We walked
You slid into and out of crisis
pain rejection seeking kindnesses
and answers that you will not yet accept.

You stood at the far end of the corridor,
let us walk to you. In tears.
And a shameless smile for me when all your hugs were done.
Welcome inside outsider.

In the back seat en route and from, your sons
and daughter bicker, tease and fight for place.
You had your place in them and him until he died on you
and they awayed in time.
So now you flap like an empty bag,
a useless womb, an impotent appendage limp and desolate.
There is no hermitage.
This corridored entanglement so beautifully landscaped
spun with Rousseau, Monet and Van Gogh
(I stared and stared Del Rio's paracletes).

Talking to you, listening, watching without seeming to
seems therapy for us, not you.
You know your answers, not their execution
— death bags no fears once you have been so close —
they haven't yet absorbed the question.
Is it not strange how separate we are — us mothers,
fathers, sons and daughters. Cataclysms isolate
and fuse. (We knife our mothers in the back
and rape their daughters)
Resting on your back in your room
you began to talk your story.
Bony fingers plucked needlessly at the neat expensive collar
of your unbuttoned blouse. I flicked my eyes to please.
I stared at clustered parrots by Del Rio
until I felt your eyes demanding explanations.

And then we waved through two glass doors
and said how good you were today
And drove away.

## Journey

I want to find my way without your help
Time I switched sides and led.
Following is wearying now,
one time great
I have no Jesus footsteps in my sands.

It rained today. I did not feel angry.
I made myself a salad plate
and toast with peanut butter.
I wrote — o! ten pages of words.

They all originally said
    'Wish we were here'.

## My Brother's Room

Cock o' the roost upon your curved legged coffee table
focuses the room upon itself: porcelain, fantailed
white and timid dove.

In memory you imply of a white pigeon
that came to visit, stayed.

Only the familiar Office bindings say 'priest'.
The rest is secular.

I used to know these rooms
and recall proclamation.
I like your silent comfortable calm.
The peace that speaks within your eyes
is here beneath this ticking clock.

I would find a pathway too, my brother.
But I do enjoy
    self-doubt, and stray.

## On a Train To New York City

On a train to New York City
buried among the trees in Metuchen
an overhead railway-car
concrete platform, blazing advert
calling me to go — go — go —

Keys — everyone sports a bunch of keys, or two,
cars in parking lots huddling in together
car-streamers on the motorways

The heat is getting to me — I thought
all America was air-conditioned.
Trim parks and trees and timber homes,
car-washes, flags and cable stringing everywhere.
Union this and union that;
black & blue —a musical review, Sarafina
Highway Pacific Coast, King of the Hill and Parliament
 Lights.
Right. New York ahead.

In among the fuel-tanks and railway girders
the next carriage is 'cold in there'
'It's cold in there — hot in here. I guess
hot is better.' Not a smile.
Don Quixote would have relished
all those pylons standing open-legged
shapeless, everywhere. And in the hazy sky
the empire state says 'watch ME'.
I watch
passing over the higher twins. Form is power.

Tunnel in through darkness. Cool breeze.
I want to tunnel too.
America sits before me in tight bright body
clinging shirt and skirt and high-heeled shoes.
Bosombound,
tight and bursting forth.

Doors unslide apart,
and noises zoomburst technicolours
through my life.

## On the steps at New York Public Library

On the steps at New York Public Library on 5th Avenue
I waited.
Three black girls talking wildly, laughing
screaming happy gesturings
in the cooler pm breeze
and their lips were pursing dreams.

Earlier
I stole glances left & right to faces
searching monitors in the catalogue corner
thoughtful energetic faces, elixir to my me.
Watching makes me much more randy
than a 42nd video.

When the train is late, there still is time
to reach your destination.
Your flight is now. You have to go.
I too have made commitments.
say hallo —
    Goodbye.

## Metropark, New Jersey

At Metropark, NJ
I hoped that you would sit by me
with that white smile and those black eyes
shining with being pleasure.
But you chose the empty seat in front.
Was that so I could watch your face?
Train whistle blew
and when I looked again
you had gone, sending me alone
to Washington, DC.

## A Daddy Bewildered

We think our children
    wonders of this universe
and lose our awesome selves
    in service of their beauties.
They pinch each tear before it forms
    and drain each courage dry
with laughter, style and childer-ness.
They makes us bounce with pride at their varieties.

Daughter — son
    Son — daughter
How I love you unknown to all myself!
You seed my drills and harrow down my angers —
But still, my loves, be still:
    I have another question ...

How can I love you
    more than me?

For me,
    your past is all now.
For you,
    I am your history.

## My Treat

I brought my kids to the British Museum
after a long day city sighting.
It seemed to be a mistake but I needed the visit.
They gave me two hours out of their holiday.
That was generous. I tried my best — sphinxes,
hieroglyphics, statues, stories. Interest died.
Boring, bores, bores. Let's go daddy.
My own feet were tired, but how could I give in?

When we met a reconstructed Grecian temple
adventure generated energy.
[I've never understood what it had been
but wish I could bottle it]
Next door, the Elgin Marbles. I asked
the fading eyes for five minutes,
reluctantly conceded — plus a coke.

It seems the text inspired a game
for twenty minutes later when I called out time
they begged five minutes to complete the hall!
I bargained for a visit to the mummy room.

They got angry there that mummy children
and the mummy women — breasts identified —
should have been museumed
[no comment nor acknowledgement of mummy men]
I held my daughter close and silly said
'I prefer those women ones, don't you?'
Her eyes alighted swift on mine
and whispered — 'Coke.'

# Bird in a Vacuum Pump

*An Experiment [Painted in 1768 by Joseph Wright]*

Daddy — will it die?
— Maybe.
Don't do it, Dad.
— I must. I need to know.
No, Daddy, no.
— Don't be silly child.
I'm not silly! It's cruel.
— No love, it's not cruel. The bird will feel no pain. It will just die — and go to the birds' heaven.
D A D D Y !!
— Here, hold this down and watch. If the bird can't fly, I will have proved a vacuum here. A step for mankind, for the future. Look, look!
— There!
— What?
Stop it. Stop it Daddy, it's not dead.
— I can't, love. Here help me with this pump.
Do it yourself, Dad.
— Hey, come back here you!
— Shit. — Bloody children!

## Child Asleep

Those words I heard addressed to me
    were never spoken.
I have tasted all the shadows in your hair.
I waited by the stairs to follow
thinking I could sense your calling
    asking me to come.

When I ventured later on to hug goodnight
You were mysteriously asleep.

Once, halfway up the stairs
    I hesitated on the fifth step;
a disconcerted realising that there is no centre.
My fiftieth birthday still someways away.

A wedge of torn wallpaper creviced by the next generation
lay poorly camouflaged to my experienced eye.
Proclaiming as the stoned slabs of Inismor
that cliff armoured plateaus sea to sky,
an aged skin ripened to be shed
all unencumbered
by the bridles of the past.

Those soils have loosened to the wind
their flavours and their juices and their seeds;
they have absorbed and polished stone,
and they no longer serve.
Is this the future cast,
    the place to come,
the land to be, the fullness
    generations cannot see?

And five more steps to go for me:
I taste the vibrance of this air
I have remembrances to share
and all those dreams still shadowed
in the lair of our unventured ways
awaiting centres to unfold and hold me.

And yes, I can see
the very top step of this stairs.

## Wordwaiting

While waiting for some words to come
and give me entrance to a poem for you
I idle through the room, filling with its clutter.

Tidier than yours, my Friend. Tidier than yours!

And a thought — that almost passed unhitched — said:
If I drop dead, if I drop dead
all of these papers, notes, files and books
bills and documents, rubber stamps and pens; souvenirs
of distant echoes — spears and fly-whisks, Chagga bowls,
Ngoni blanket bark, photos, everlasting flowers from Kibo's
alpine slopes; briefcaseholdingwork, lovenotes hidden
in unsafe corners even I have now forgotten; calculators, dictaphone
with tapes unfilled; novels, books, fine editions, poems and poems and more

— Oh my god just one wee room to endlessly spin on this jetsamflotsam...

— if I dropped dead right now, not one piece here would matter to me then;

I would be GONE.

Tell me:
what might you find to help me live on?

# A Final Fling

*The young people are very peaceful.*
                        Lu Hsun, 'Hope' *in* Wild Grass

My heart is — extraordinarily —
void of love and hate, sadness, colour, sound or joy.
I am growing old.
It is true, my hair is going white. If so,
my soul's hair is surely whitening too?

But did I not grow old one hundred years ago?

Before that my heart was full of iron song,
passion's blood and fight and fall and resurrection
until one day it abandoned me.
I think it was some woman was the cause
for it happened after one had given up
on my immobility. But even so, it came
and all that I have left is hope,
a shield against the dark night's love of fear
hanging on my body's walls.
Hope, and behind it youth and otherness.

O, I remember moonlight, stars and butterflies,
owls in flowers and laughter —
It was not how I see it now from this hopeless hillock;
[why is it so? Is it that all the young people
of the world have grown old before me?
and become anxious for life's maternities.]
'Despair, like hope,' my good friend, dead, assured me,
'is just another vanity.'
Is it not sad that his memory is still alive in me.

He should be all forgotten
to round off this once-ness.

I would have a last great fling in my old age.
Even if I cannot find the youth outside.
They sit calmly on the college greens, thinking time away.
They do not see my fight.
Surely they will rise in angered love,
destroy, create, re-live, re-die?

— Arise!

I can hear my hollow mucus tubes
frightening the lives out of everyone
as they wait for me to go.
They do not seem to know that this is my last great fling,
this surging deeply gasping breathing
searching everywhere for air.
I know those ugly sounds so full and live to me.
Inward — snortings, gurglings, scrapings;
outward — hisses as this great gasbag husky hollow
    diseased chest
deflates ... I will not let it go — it go — it go ...
Time has gone now. There is only massive breathings,
and my mind. I do not find — I cannot summon — god
to hedge my bets. So, this is how I go ... go ...
And my heart is full of an extraordinary loneliness
and there is no one there to know.
I cheer. To cheer. To go ... to go ... I... GO —

## Lutan Baba

to all our handclapped rhythms of prayer and celebration
to the silence of desert trails and mountain tracks
to the hum chug threats of car and truck
to the lift and twist of elbowed knee
to the pain of open wounds on me
to the beat of silent dreams — roll on.

Roll on Baba, I was there to see you
roll along our planet crust and make us tracks for peace.

At the crossroads one of many I was there
watching with the curious and committed
the victims and the dead, your sweet agenda.
And we dreamed of whirring dervishes
of jumping warriors headbutting cloudy skies; or ballet
    dancers gracing nocturnes out of *Field* by Chopin —
    hauntingly insidious among the rocks and dirt and
    crevices of your long route
through hell and smell and clayey nodes.

matted hair and body baited; free of pain so full of it
only a mind to drive it on beyond
the barriers of masks put on.

Roll on Lutan Baba, turn and gyre upon this ground
roll along our planet crust and make us tracks for peace

to all our handclapped rhythms of prayer and celebration
to the silence of desert trails and mountain tracks

to the hum chug threats of car and truck
to the lift and twist of elbowed knee
to the pain of open wounds on me
to the beat of silent dreams — roll on.

[Afternotes:
Hounds of heaven — whirling dervishes in Turkey — 13th century
Muslim — Lutan Baba 20th-century India — for peace bypassing
Punjab — fear of terrorism — gurus and disciples — Jesuses great and
small — garlanded with saffron flowers — oranges and greens — Masai
warriors — hearing Chopin who took John Field's nocturne and
developed something 'hauntingly beautiful' gyre — wandering monks,
rotating bodies, Yeatsian placing, rebirthing holiness]

## The Seven Masks of Tone LaGee

Tone LaGee's seven masks have come undone

pride
   covetousness
               lust
                    anger
                          gluttony
                                  envy
                                       sloth

I must ask.
Whose heart is caked in such absorbing powers?
How does it cope? How can it care?
I must see.

> He wants his pride; he covets greater things;
> He love his lusts; he thrives in angers;
> Occasional gluttonies massage his agonies;
> He envies those who never envy him;
> In sloth he finds extraordinary shafts of life ...

Good god, that collar he took off shook off those seven masks
yet all their flavours seeped absorbed intrigued
and left within one hidden mask of fear,
the sweet heart of jesus stuffed with rabid sweetmeats,
giblets untainted by the truths proclaimed.
'Divorce me from the tinctured bloods and offals of my stark philosophies,' he prayed;
'and toss me into some fired ceramic kiln to burn my ether free.'

Tone LaGee would be free of you,
free of branded supermarket gods for centuries proclaiming
pride, covetousness, lust, anger, gluttony, envy, sloth
— all for the glory of his sometime god.

Such deadly weapons — he reflected — for fashioning human history
and all its ignominy, all its glory,
still hail him now, enough to fill confessionals
long thwarted by clowns and acrobats miming their silent ecstasies on sawdust floors.
Perhaps he too should leave the back row, the company of family,
the cheering ticket holders in the stalls, the happy innocence of front row seats
and join those clowns and acrobats to carnival with song and dance
and solemn grounded celebration.

Tone LaGee will dance with you; dally with me.
Will lust and strut, fight and steal, cheat and smile
and ask his god to rest a while
and let the world flow free.
Tone LaGee will bend a knee to promises
Will browse and prise philosophie;
will rage and till and bend at will
his earth-god's window-sill.

## Cursor

the cursor on my screen tells me get on with it
the cursor in my mind ditto
my heart too
my eyes search
my ears hear
my fingers touch
my tongue tastes

yet i am
        dead
                silent
                        blank
static
        nowhere

the cursor blinks and makes me
        angry
                awake
                        warm
moving
alert
lost

where is there a way to get around
those blank spaces in the mind
where is there a way to overcome
the cold valves of the heart
where is there a way to restore
the lost heavens of decades past dreaming
where

o where
o where
come sit by my side and tell me
come with me
come to me
come for me

kiss me

give me your silence over mine
slip your angers under mine
tell me all tell me all tell me all
tell me
tell

# Versifying Verses, 1–4

*Verse 1 (1.1.1996)*

To be loved is the beginning of loving
To be chaste is a test of stamina
To have nothing to say is justification for silence
To say it suggests the abyss of lovelessness.
A sensitivity to drafts under doors and through closed windows
Might give reason to search for cracks in the walls
But unless you repair them, or slip through them,
Your knowledge sits like dandruff on your scalp
Growing itself into itchiness.
And what will you do — scratch?


*Verse 2 (2.1.1996)*

Giving and receiving may reveal balances
Hidden day to day.
The child on Christmas night
Exploring the cardboard packaging,
And tinsel on the tree;
New sweater, underwear and ties
Neatly folded in the right presses
To await discovery and understanding;
A gift of flowers without a card
A silent tear.

*Verse 3 (3.1.1996)*

Each year at this time
Driven by obsession with completions
I re-read my workday diary notes.
In there find all sorts of petty crimes and unsolved
    mysteries,
minor disasters, more minor triumphs, deaths, and
    sometime blessings
As I page by page through January to now.

The blessings are my blank pages.
They give me pause — overwork, or travel,
Or forgetfulness — and hope:
Perhaps, a moment in history, intensely felt, achieved,
Not needing for its future recollection
The banality of diary pages cataloguing shelves of
    mediocrity.
Who knows?

*Verse 4 (1.5.1996)*

This is May.
Lady day.
Where have March and April gone? No song ...
There is no poem on the file, not one blank space in
    kilobytes.
My forehead heavy and my shoulders droop, my eyes
faintly sting from endless undigested lettuces.

This                    cyberspace
        is                        tempting ...

## When a Friend died ...

Lying there.
Egyptian
kind of
alive in death.
I had to touch your cheek

in disbelief
princess
idea-full
now emptiness
you had abandoned us.

I came alone
to this mahogany
sombre-suited vestry
host
to your deathly pearl

Alone I waited
waited
knowing
waited
said goodbye
and kissed your forehead.

Outside
Aungier street
bustled about my waiting
till a taxi came
to take me to our other world
now without you.

And I think
how all my thoughts of you
unfold inside
and sometimes blossom
sometimes tell me I will die.

## Remembering Daddy

Ten years is a long time to be dead, Dad.
I wonder if you knew when going that it was for ever.
   For ever!
I don't know what it means to talk to you now — although
   I do —
nor did I then. I remember silences, and later small talk,
and never ever big talk, deep talk, love talk. What a son!
When you got a stroke, I remember trying to connect
my mind to yours — without much real success for me,
although perhaps sensing something real for you
was my pride, and not your gain, your smile, your pain.

Good god, you taught me some stuff! — learning off by
   heart
times-tables, catechism answers, poems — making traps
for lady wagtails, blackbirds, sparrows down our garden,
pyramids of elder sticks and twine.
Gallogs made tyre-strip springy catapults,
shoe-tongue'd bootlace slingshots
practised on our Laxton-superbs.

I was afraid, you know. Like 'Fear of God'.
But that was my child.
And later, your focus
seemed to embrace but never know my interests,
seemed to pride in just being — yours, and also mine.
Now
I look at me and see some chastening parallels — or is it
consequences, generation-transfers on my soul?

Yes, I've brought them — sons and daughters — to your
 grave.

Still, my sisters insist I had the best time — got my way.
And so I must have for I was a good boy.
And now wish I had been bad too. Black sheep can
 memoir.

I dreamed a song the other night. It was called
 'Remembering Daddy' — full with
rhyme and rhythm, hope and time.
By morning it had disappeared, but I still knew
that in remembering you, I was remembering me.

This is not that dreamsong, but perhaps
it will become my way to still the air,
my opening of remembrance,
my prayer.

## Great Hungry Poets

Was it famine made our poets' voices great,
our great poet-songs;
Or were they always?

Are you hungry now
for chips with salt and vinegar
to fill your mouth and burn
your tongue driving with one hand on a wheel?

I thought so.
Think too of simpler loves
of words of nourishment
pain a poem-abandoned home.

# In a stormy place

*[on reading Wendell Berry's 'Elgy']*

We went home to Conna after Christmas
to mother days as every year, eating, reminiscing.
Saturday morning — kids in bed — give hours for breakfast talk
of childhood as a winter storm tossed skies, give trees cries
of pain at ice-cold raindrops showering chill and swirling January gusts.
Mammy had the room fire set since eight, the milk and morning paper bought,
and the bread ready to toast at the sound of my feet on the stairs.

By half past ten my children came — and went —
preferring Granny's television to breakfast and knowing well
a tray will soon appear their morning tastes catered for.
Grannies do that. Children know.

I wanted to visit Daddy's grave before rain set the day.
They had always come — to help me pray, to find
the drama of all the dead people in their breasts,
to ask questions put each visit for the answers:
can he hear us? [giggled]; is God here? did you love your Daddy?
Who put the flowers there, Granny? Why? Isn't she 80?
Can we go now?

This time I am alone. With coat and umbrella, a brisk walk
past post-office, Goughs, dispensary, new terrace to the hall

its forties deco'd frontage a semi-strident pink, clean and familiar,
backstage extended now to tennis court, sports centre
— no disrespect to the old ball-alley.
Threatening skies promised winter cloudbursts.

As gaps of sunlight disappeared and half the heavens dimmed
At the gates of Conna castle, on the New Line
the rain began, the wind beyond gale force wrassled, whistled, hummed
rushing through the roadline trees and shiver branches.

The skies were urging me stand clear, crouch down, hide
from forces there beyond the touch and taste of man.
The radio had warned of eighty-mile-an-hour winds. This must be it.

Standing by my father's grave I seemed to have invented for myself
this gothic scene indulged in by the skies above;
I used to ache at the bareness of his name and lifetime on the plinth
bringing with them slips of memory — but with no grip.
This time I was more conscious of a shifting wind.

Has it been too long for sadness? Is all I am transmitted,
and these remains mere traces of a man?

I walked back home as clouds unburdened ice-cold hail;
winds bit vibrant at my face; umbrella ribbed by gale
absorbing wild energies and in my self a calm undone.

Memory a dream dog calling to some moon.

# The Whole Universe is up for Grabs

Sitting here, in the Extension waiting
157 e-mails flickering to my screen
from 'titanic-discuss' telling me things I will not be told
my eyes siding to wind-blown sheets and shirts
and evening darkness closing down the day's grey sky,
I wonder were I dead now
how long my presence would overhang this place, my
    House.

And not for long I reflect as I sense me clinging for a
    while —
not on my own recognisance but lingering
heavily and solemnly in my children's minds
— such sadness they will not have felt before:
why do we leave this cloud —
why not be happy — happy times remembered?
Perhaps later — but by then my connections will have gone
and I will have been nothingness for sure.

Maybe you will read a poem of mine,
or you, child-woman-man, recollect some fine event that
    logged on mind.
But that is not me is it? That is you shaping me for your
    present
where there is now for me no tangibility — just ghostly
    shadow tainted
memory, feathering mind-entrapped possession.
My e-mails get a second chance before consignment to
    oblivion.

I play god and say die! no care where the noughts and ones
 be?
like the great god, spaceless mystery.
There was no beginning:
— for if so then there be god;
but if no — with or without me —
the whole universe is up for grabs
and I just want it now all for myself.

# The Stoker on the Rim

On browsing *Father Browne's Titanic Album*

— 1 —

It is I who grins down upon the whole world.
From atop this elegant stack of life, above, beyond
wave and tide, hills low-lying past my harbour,
looking back now, forward, back again
my face unable to restrain the dream within.
I am going where great imaginings can be
beyond the hope of everyman to dream about.
I am on my way and leave behind the great abyss
of history, and mine.

I will leave legends — smiling nodes,
threatening waves, collision bursts and truth.
for in my dying here above, behind all I see
are silent faces holding to the sea.

— 2 —

There is power in the chug drumming chugging
and fire in the faces of men shovelling coal
and heat burning knuckles and coal
and the black and the white and the red orange glow
knot gruntings and laughings and curses to coal.

These are my great infernal machines.
Progress and power and heat, mighty heat.

Heave through the wavebodies thundering water
Smile at the sweat-licking muscle-ing load
And people and people and people to goad!

We drive through the ocean's whitechurning waters
and watery calms and their silences true, and
long for the shores that lie over horizons
but want not to reach them for fear of their holds.
And we shovel and sweat and test our emotion.

I call to you friends as you search for me here
too far from the land, too near to the sea:
just watch my departure become an arrival
my journey to new ports and new worlds and places
that have waited expectant, long waited for me.

I go now, I go, I love you, goodbye.
Sail on Mr Smith! New World — Ahoy!

# The Man who tried to sell Dublin to the Bolsheviks

*In memory of Liam and Kitty*

I knew that man — and though not too old yet
am carried through him back to 1922 —
by the sharp edge of our century —
I see him differently but saw too
the lean man with furtive eyes
wearing a shabby trench-coat
a revolver strapped between his shoulderblades.
So, he said, so it is written; so it shall be done.

He was the man, they said, that tried to sell Dublin to the Bolsheviks,
locked up the unemployed in a maternity hospital
shot them unless they spat upon the crucifix.
He was a maker of myths, a man of hope, abandoned.
Not only God but too the Revolution, dead!
He nudged a comrade and said:
'There's nothing more.'

I travelled once with him to the rocky place
where he made a TV recorded visit (and farewell)
and watching him still by the wall of Kilmurvey bay;
wondered at immensity. His eyes sought a rock.
Tides wash through him now.

Or is he still listening, standing in the wings,
indifferent to the miming actors.
Eighty-eight and silent but for random bursts of song
And Kitty in the wings;

or questions stared from brightlit blue-cold eyes.
He says, 'Kitty, let's get the hell out of here'
and turns away from home.

It is curious how deep and distant
memory divines.

His visit casts new stories to re-tell,
and gives me the man to fix within the myth
of his own place. He knew the rock
where old men sat and spoke to it,
and gave it voice once more.

As the black soul dies, rockflowers bloom
and brine hisses high into the firmament
of minds attuned to the savage crash of cliff wave.

In death, demonic spirits claimed his soul
But through my angers I could only hear the laughter
and refrain coming from his front room:
'For I know it doesn't matter any more.

...

I know it doesn't matter any more.'

## While you were Out there

*13 February 1998. a Friday.*

While you were out there
filling the shadows with personality
I hid here beneath the slip hoping
tides would come and go
unremarkably.
Crouched like some wraith in a famine corner
un-live, un-dead, unimaginably curious
of the surge and slap of wave and wall,
my mind slipped
through that hesitation that said
do not go quietly
into someone else's hidey-hole; you're on your own.

I wondered if those words might be my stepping stones
or if with Gulliver, I should parade across the sea
hauling fleets of verbs to make my challenge.

Sometimes a star that falls at night
to flaunt itself
will make me angry at the space it backwashes
with questions I ignore.

I want to fly between discoveries,
I want to breathe easily and deep of me
while still I can, before my tide
turns cold and wildly goes
overboard lost in itself.

You see, while you were out there,
I stood still to watch, to admire,

and I lost time.
So if I run away and hide elsewhere remember too
I have my own shadows to compass.

The fill and fuss of kitchen chore and washing line
cutting grass, chimney sweeping, changing oil,
and talk
obscure the rush to close.

I hear you call. I see you fall.
I touch and feel and smell
the musk of thought released to cover us
indulgently. I savour certainty.

I do not surrender to my own lies.
I will die and be nothing. So this case I pile up
against my defence will be:

three things greater than things that are:
    me
    you
and, our shadows — etched on night —
setting the morning star.

## I Think My Mind Can Blossom

I think that my mind can blossom
like the lotus
drawing to its soft sweetened centres
honey bees and icicles.
Is it like this
to whom I press my lips?
I wonder as my tongue tastes
and my palms tingle
if this is love or loving lust.

How can I begin to shape
out of the emptiness within
words with any touch of reverence?

My love, I call. My love. But is it I
or is it you I love, and who are you
to rack me so, to spin my body
in its ever seeking.
Which are the pleasures of the soul?
— those ecstasies that blossom guilt
and sing melodies of beaten gold?
Which are the pleasures of the soul?
— those crocuses and orchids in your hair
[I put them there]
opening to my searching eyes.
Which are the pleasures of your soul?
— my touching you and being here
to offer us our prayers.

And what of angels singing psalms
that move our tendernesses into tears
so we can sip each other's fears?
And what of demons jabbing spears of fire
[up our sweetened rears]
bringing us to tears and filling up our tongues
with blood and waste and septic pusses?

Are these your chains of penitential treasures
binding us together?
I think my love can blossom
like the lotus in your hair
but O my heart seems chiselled out of granite stone.
My love is marrow — trapped in bone.

## Clown Faces

behind clown faces pulled at morning
bathroom mirrors touched at night
smiles for convenience
kisses for habit
hugs for not knowing the words

hop, skip and hop down streets
slouch laneways home?
drop bombs on Kosovars
and live the lotto week.

indeed a worthy citizen,
in your role, off the dole
being nice.

have you ever noticed how the world
of busy people busy every day
at play at work at work at home
is mirrored in the night
plucking eyebrows, trimming nostrilhairs
and teasing disconcerting spores.

The light in Connemara,
so I'm told,
is wondrously precise for painting.

## Carnival Clowns & Acrobats

When the carnival came, nobody noticed what was missing.

There was a wonderful Prologue telling all how rooted in time and place we are, — paddling under bridge eyes, touching river fish, breaking stones, dreaming of distant silent lands not really that far off, reaching out to darkest Africa and further back to Amergin, Poet of Poets.

And then came the Intermission filled with voice of audience participant in magic dreams, first loves and special things ...

Quickly to an Epilogue where wise men stuttered over crates emptied of words we could understand, and shadows were cast upon the songs of the smaller gods.

The carnival was over, heroes identified, baby born ...

Alas — where was the substance that the children of the earth must want: — the clowns and acrobats, the elephants and prancing ponies, the ferocious mammals tamed by dark courageous trainers, trapeze wonder-leaps and grand masters cracking whips.

When my children began to hang up the phone on me, I came to appreciate the fullness of love. But left to my own devices, crises needed to re-discover become my carnival.

So — might I bring on clowns and acrobats to perform for
you?
They fill my heart with joy — wet my eyes embarrassingly
at times. But they are all that I seem to have and hold:
my business deals are done; my friends are met; my
family nurtured; and I? Still searching canvas tents for
tearholes leading to a sky I know to be outside.
In here I still lack the courage to swipe away my face
paints.